Competing As a Lifestyle

You vs You

A student's guide to greatness!!!

Competing as a Lifestyle:
You vs You
A Student's Guide to Greatness

Printed in the United States of America

ISBN-13: 978-0615886053

Competing As a Lifestyle

You vs You

A student's guide to greatness!!!

The "Competing As A Lifestyle© Philosophy" is a breakthrough perspective for students to understand a great way to think while on their journey through life's race. While this is my philosophy for success, there is nothing philosophical about unleashing your potential.

There are 7 billion people in the world and yet no two set of fingerprints are alike. Sounds interesting? Should be, since no one can achieve for you what only you can achieve for yourself. What is it that you need to know to fulfill your purpose? Engage in learning, build a vision, justify discipline, embrace passion, discover who you are and build character with understanding.

In this book, I will share with you some of my most meaningful life experiences that have helped me find the answers to these questions and more. Through the ups and downs, I've learned that I can only blame myself for my failures. The battle is mine, as well as your battle is only yours. Most of the time our biggest enemy is ourselves. I realized how my poor habits, faulty thinking and generational bondage kept me from recognizing my purpose.

These principles shared with you in my book will lead you as they did me to the root cause of a lack of success in life and illuminate what is necessary for you to begin to fulfill your purpose.

Your victory will be a discovery of your passion and how to deliver your gift to the world. Don't give up! We all need you!

Competing As a Lifestyle
You vs You
A student's guide to greatness!!!

Dedications

Job Corps Students

Thank you to the students of Job Corps. Over the last four years you have taught me the true meaning of endurance. Many of you are overcoming severe obstacles that would have forced the average person to give up. Watching you grow and desire a better future for your families was a great experience for me. It is my hope that you continue to grow in strength and knowledge so you can position yourselves to achieve enormous success. Don't get complacent in your academic pursuits. Aim for perfection in everything you do. Understand that you are the next generation of Americans to lead us into the future. While building your dreams you have to know your true value and demand full payment from life and it will gladly pay.

My Dear Wife

Reathanak (Ra), I love you Honey. Without your love and endurance through my personal and spiritual growth, I would not be the man I am today. I know it was not always easy, but you stayed the course. Your love and faithfulness has ignited a wave of love from me to you and to humanity. I appreciate and love the fortified commitment you have for our family. You are truly a virtuous woman. *"Your children rise up and call you blessed"*.

My Parents

Mom and Dad I admire your resilience to win. You didn't leave me a million dollars, but what you gave me money couldn't. You gave me the will to win. As I reflect on the days when failure wasn't an option, you pulled us through. When I tried to give up, you wouldn't let me. When I worried, you made it happen. You taught me the power of WE! You give honor where honor is due and today I take my hat off with everyone who reads this book. Let it be written----the son of a janitor and female construction worker who broke her back to provide for her family has built a legacy to remember. We are not perfect people------ but we are ONE. Ward Nation!!!

Key Points:
- How to create a firm life **vision**. This may be the single most important portion of your journey. If you don't have a direction, how do you know what disciplines are needed?
- Understanding the disciplines needed to make your vision a reality.
- Embracing the passion that it takes to build your dream.
- Building your dream on a solid foundation, which is character.
- You vs You: This is the fight between you now and who you desire to be. To have the courage to confront this issue will put you in an uncomfortable position.
- Making good choices versus poor choices.
- Loving family through tough times.
- Embracing the nerds!! We need them.
- Having the courage to be different.

Looking for these key points in the book will produce an expectant attitude for the teachable moments in this book. Taking life ownership of these principles will set you free to reach your full potential.

How will this book help you grow?
Your social and emotional intelligence will be strengthened. You will be able to recognize situations that will not be helpful to you in building your dreams. Also, you will be able to recognize the emotions, people and thoughts that trigger the worst version of yourself. Embrace this book and let's grow together.

Chapter One: Discipline

At age 32, I heard a wise but simple saying by a man who told me I would be his janitor. He said what you don't know WILL hurt you. I am not a janitor, but had I gotten that information as a teen, or earlier, I would not have made as many mistakes as I did in the earlier stages of my life.

Former pro golfer Tom Kite said it best: "Discipline is a matter of being interested."

The early stages of our life are so important because daily actions become our habits and our habits reveal our character. Character represents who you are. It speaks for you before you show up. As a teenager, I didn't receive this kind of detailed information. I was told to play sports, do well in school and have fun.

Once I was exposed to our culture's low standards, they ate me alive. I eventually became a teen dad and I had no clue how to be a dad. By the time I was 17, I had experimented with drugs and alcohol and it was expectable behavior. The results of my habits were becoming very clear. I was heading in the wrong direction and the car I was driving didn't have brakes. I was a teen dad, school wasn't easy and I didn't have a good foundation to build a solid dream on. How could I become successful with this start? I was paying child support as a senior in high school. My friends and my family were on my side and supported me and I appreciated the support, but I wish someone would have told me what I am telling you right now: if you stay disciplined in your education, extracurricular activities (sports, clubs etc.) and morals, then you can write your own ticket. I wish someone would have had the moral courage to refuse to accept my lifestyle and had not allowed me to feel comfortable with the life that I was living.

The great Polish educator Abraham J. Heschel said: *"Self- respect is the fruit of discipline; the sense of dignity grows with the ability to say no to oneself."*

One of the most powerful life attributes we can possess is discipline. With this, our dreams feel closer. It gave me hope when there was no hope. When I couldn't trust my coach or my friends, I could trust my discipline. I would spend hours in the gym visualizing myself making game winning shots and shaking guys to get to the basket. During games, the person in front of me didn't know that I had already beaten him to the hoop a thousand times that year. Because I had already put in the work, the hard games were easy – they were the one-hour version of my personal 6-hour workouts.

I learned that if I wanted to be a professional basketball player I would need to shoot 1,000 shots a day. Coach told me I needed to lift weights to become a stronger player to compete on the next level. I would also need to be the first player in the gym and the last one to leave. If I wanted to continue to pursue my dreams of playing professional basketball, I would need to say no to myself in several areas of my life. There were times when I wanted to do the fun stuff or just go kick it, as some kids put it. But most times I couldn't do that because it would interrupt my daily self-discipline; discipline that would position me for my goals.

I had the proper discipline athletically, but academically I was a mess. I consistently maintained a "D" average in high school and I finished with a 1.9 GPA. This is where it got tricky – although I was filled with talent, I was about to attempt to go to college without making the grade. KIDS: DON'T TRY THIS AT HOME. I didn't know it, but I had just played the lottery with my future and I wasn't holding a winning ticket.

DO YOU WANT TO BE SUCCESSFUL?

Based on your actions, the conversations you've had, the music you've listened to, the television shows you've watched and the friends you've spent time with over the past week; would these activities agree or disagree with your success? Would they make you successful or hold you hostage to your circumstances?

This exercise usually exposes our poor habits. Some of these habits may not seem like they are a hindrance, but they are a complete hindrance. You have to have a clear understanding of what you are working towards. What are your priorities? Some people make nice clothes and shoes their top priority. For some people, it may be a nice car. For others, it may be living in a big home. What will you focus your discipline toward?

With the proper focus, you will reap the fruit of your labor. If the labor is a negative action, you will reap negative fruit – and you will have planted it all on your own. If you plant the proper disciplines, you will be able to eat from the tree of goodness all the days of your life. Remember, the choice is yours and you can't expect someone to always give you a warning. You are supposed to take heed and not be a follower because, sometimes, the people around you will have been stuck in life – making no progression. Understand that the people who DO take heed are often made fun of or made to feel like an outsider, but this is to be expected. The reason why it's hard to be great is because it takes courage to be different.

Courage isn't something everyone is born with. Sometimes we are lucky enough to have courageous people in our lives that we can look to for examples, but usually we learn by ourselves. This attribute is a direct result of your beliefs. Plenty of men and women have the courage to risk their lives in America by selling drugs, gang-banging and allowing themselves to end up in the belly of the beast. But if a person has the courage to do these things, they have yielded mentally to the acceptance of that lifestyle. What will your beliefs say about you? Will your beliefs lead you to that fruitful place where a young person with goals and dreams can flourish? Or will you follow the crowd and mimic others, only to be enlisted in the army of mere existence?

In order to fully use your courage to get through life, you have to have a "never-give-up" attitude. I remember when I was told it couldn't be done. I can remember when I felt like giving up, but after a while, I figured out that if I just stayed the course, I would eventually win.

"You don't have to be the best; you just have to outlast the rest." - LaMarqué Ward, Sr.

You can't let self-defeating thoughts enter your brain. For every thought you have of failure, you have to have three reasons why you can make it. I have never seen anyone lose a three-on-one game in sports or in life. So in order to put that much positive reinforcement in your mind, you have to limit your intake of negativity (music, television, family, friends, etc.). Every day you have to create intentional actions because you are either building success or moving backwards – there is no in-between. I have noticed that a lot of people who are underachievers have attempted to create this "chill" place, but it is not real. The people who buy into this thinking will just exist, until they expire, unless they wake up from their slumber. The sad part about this is that once you get in, it is like playing the lottery to get out of this way of thinking. And how many people do you know who have played the lottery their whole lives and have never won? Imagine getting sucked into a place like that.

"The brain can be likened to a garden and if you sow good seed it will bring forth good fruit. If you sow bad seed it will bring forth bad fruit." - James Allen

Your brain is the control tower. Isn't it funny that God put the three ways we feed ourselves on our head. **Hint; hint**...your brain is the control tower. If you have more negative going in than positive, you might have a negative world view or you might be self deceived into believing you're normal, but your life will never materialize into the grand vision you think you deserve because your habits won't steer you in the right direction.

To build a strong foundation for a great life, you will need to apply these principles, if you want to receive the return on your life investment later down the road. Young people irrationally think the biggest decisions they will have to make will be made once they get older, but I beg to differ.

Your educational habits are what get you through the loops of life and allow you to be enlightened to go through the proper doors. Your willingness to dream will focus you on things that are much larger than you. This will allow you to borrow the strength that you will need from tomorrow to get through today. Your courage to be different and stand strong in the face of jokes and loneliness will move you through the rest of your life.

The more you read, the more you learn – but you can't focus your disciplines in a few areas. You want to create a balanced life. When you are able to create discipline in your faith, family, friends, finances and fun – you can separate yourself from everyone. How many teenagers are thinking about attempting to manage all of these areas with commanding ownership? It's easy to let your responsibility of one of these key areas of your life be given to someone else around you. When that happens, the decision at that time may not be in your best interest. The pressures that the average young person faces make it easy to forfeit the responsibility. It's easy to have a "go-with-the-flow" attitude and to be a follower because "everyone else is doing it." I beg you not to allow this to happen to you. You can't control everything, but if you can plan, prepare and have the courage to face these areas every day with a never-give-up attitude, over time you will win.

There is no excuse for an excuse. Everyone has a reason why they couldn't get it done. One time I missed my family pictures and my wife was not happy with me. I was going to Myrtle Beach the next morning and I had to pick up some marketing material at the last minute. She waited on me and I never made it to the photo shoot. Later she called me and gave me an ear full and I deserved it. She expected me to give her a logical excuse, but I refused to try to rationalize my blunder. I said, "Honey, I had to help them prepare my material and I did not plan on it. I am sorry." She tried to get me to give her a reasonable excuse that she could live with and I refused to make up something that was "good enough." She went to Panera bread and read her bible and came home later. When she came home she didn't even mention it.

"Discipline is the bridge between you and your goals." -Jim Rohn

When nothing else works, you can count on your habits to get you through. One day you will look back and see how you are reaping the fruit of your habits from five or ten years ago. This is why you should never give up. When you are not fruitful, wisdom says it is a time to sow good seed. When you learn to sow good seeds, whether you are up or down, then you will never run out of fruit. If discipline is not a part of your core principles of life, you will never get what you need out of life. Systems change, but principles don't.

This is why it is good for your educational aspirations to be a pursuit. When you begin to seek the proper information, you will be enlightened beyond your years and the benefits of your pursuit will reward you.

Discipline in thoughts is very important for a young person. You can't let others manipulate your mental strength. When you allow others to make you feel angry, sad or depressed you have given them total control over you. You have to reclaim those rights by being consistent in the right areas of your life. You have to have the courage to be willing to stand-a l o n e . Remember, people don't like change. If you get the big idea to decide to change your life for the better, it may not be well received from others. This may include family members. If your family doesn't support you, don't take it personally. They may not understand at the time, but they will be there with you at the end. One thing that I have found to be a good habit is to take time to sit alone to ponder my thoughts and assess myself – and this can work for you as well. Due to the nature of our fast- paced lives, there is rarely a moment when we are not receiving some type of message. We have social networking sites like Twitter, Facebook or MySpace linked to our phones. We are constantly receiving updates of what everyone else is thinking, but we never take the time to update ourselves by being still. If you take the time to be still, you will gain the ability to measure your thoughts and kick out what doesn't make sense. You have to be in control of your thoughts. If you take the time to master yourself, this pursuit will be one of the most notable pursuits you have ever pursued.

"The first and best victory is to conquer self." - Plato

Nerds

The smart kids catch a hard time in school. Their discipline is so rare at their age that they don't fit in. Our culture is so mob driven that these kids are rarely noticed. They are driven to the edge of the playground so people like me can feel halfway normal. These kids are so brilliant they could probably be the teacher's assistant, but no one will admit to it. Because they are so smart, we label them dumb. As time passes by and they find their sweet spot, they turn into people like Bill Gates. Without these people, what would our world be like?

I have some advice for you. Respect and be nice to these people because they own the companies those other kids work for. In school, their brain was just ahead of its time. You will get there as well, but we all are on an IEP (Individual Education Plan). I learned this from my own personal education process. I was not a very good student until after I turned 25. Now I pursue information like it is food for the day. We all have seasons in life and you have to learn when it is time to till the ground, sow seed and harvest it. Promise me that you will look out for these people and help them along their way because just like we need you, we need them as well. When you get a little older you will think back on the nerds and be grateful for their contributions.

Delayed gratification is a mindset and it is not normal today. Most people want some form of reward right now. We live in a microwave generation. But if you can get the reward today for your work, then you're not working for the right things – and you are probably pretty selfish. People who work for larger accomplishments can't receive the reward up front because when you shoot for the moon, you make so many mistakes along the way that you spend a large majority of your time trying to fix your mistakes. It may take you a little more time, but when you make it to the moon I would like to think you can enjoy that. You have to believe in something that is pulling you towards it, in order to have great discipline and work hard for delayed gratification. Things that are that large are purpose issues. When you are done, people will remember your name.

Doesn't this get you excited? I told a group of young people that I want to work so hard and build such a good name for my family that my great grandchildren will be able to get a meal off of my name. This is why I say that you should chase your passions. Do the thing that sets your heart on fire when you think of it. Even if I couldn't receive the reward for 10 years, I would be happy doing it. What else matters?

Family

One area in which young people often lack discipline is the family. You have to know that no parent sets out to mess up your childhood. Parents make mistakes just like young people and they have to deal with the consequences of their actions. I can remember my wife telling me how her parents never put them in programs, sports or after-school activities and she felt like it hindered them because they missed out on several opportunities in life. So for years she has carried this horrible burden and her parents didn't even know she felt this way.

We have little children and she is committed to put them in everything. My daughter plays the harp and my wife told the harp teacher the story about her childhood, possibly looking for an agreement of some sort about the importance of childhood activities. The teacher, a wise and sweet older woman, told my wife that her parents were probably busy trying to put food on the table. This was not the answer she was looking for, but it turned the light bulb on in her mind. This moment changed her perspective about her childhood and set her free from that burden.

For years I carried around the hurt of the things that my parents shouldn't have taught me and could have taught me, but as I got older I could say that my parents gave me their best. Now I am obligated to do the same for my family. Were things perfect? No!!! But my parents never gave up. They worked hard and never made excuses. My mom taught us to never be a giverupper.

Giverupper- A person who consistently resists change to maintain their current status and blames their issues on others.

She instilled hope in us. I will never forget the day we didn't have any food and I asked her what we were going to eat and she looked at me and said, "Baby, when I start worrying you start worrying."

Yes, we did eat dinner that night. What I am saying is in all of our families there is good and bad, but when you look over your life later you will see the honest effort of your family to propel you ahead of them. So open your eyes and run your race now. How can you be disciplined with your family? Honor your parents, no matter what your opinion is about them and be gracious with everyone else. Things always change. You only get one family and when they are gone you can't get time back. Finally, you need to be humble. Learn from their mistakes, improve on their wisdom and be grateful for life, health and strength.

Chapter One Questions

1. What did you learn about discipline in this chapter?

_____
_____
_____
_____
_____

2. Write three ways you can be more disciplined in your current personal and academic goals:

_____
_____
_____
_____

3. When rating yourself on your current state of discipline and measuring yourself to only the best in your selected career or goals, what would be your rating? 10 being the best and 1 being the worst:

_____
_____
_____
_____

4. If your current discipline could label you with three words, what would they be? (Example: hard working, lazy)

_____
_____
_____
_____

Chapter Two: Vision

How can you get anywhere if you don't know where you're going? Too often, our young people run wild and turn to negative things because they lack focus on their future. This might happen because the adults around them are not following a clear vision for *their* personal lives. As a result, our youth are tricked – not by the *words* of those adults, but by their **actions**. Our youth need to see solid, consistent examples of people executing, following and living a great vision for their lives.

"A big enough DREAM will be a sedative to the pain and disappointment of the journey of life." - LaMarqué Ward, Sr.

My Dream was to play in the NBA – and athletically, I was great. I achieved the top 100 in the nation as well as the prestigious McDonald's All- American nominee status. But I hated school. I was a teen dad who was finishing high school with a 1.9 GPA. When I earned my diploma, I could have chosen to give up on school because I didn't like it, but I had a larger dream: I wanted to go to college to play basketball. And as a by product of me chasing my dream, I picked up an associate's degree and I earned a bachelor's degree from Fairleigh Dickinson University.

I still hadn't become a fan of the educational process and I wasn't equipped with the skills to really excel academically, but no matter how painful the process, I was still willing to go through it to reach my goal of playing in the NBA. So as I stumbled through my academic college career, I bulldozed through my athletic career.

After finishing FDU, I hadn't finished all my requirements for my degree – but I earned my basketball degree and I went to play ball overseas. I did this for about four years. Although finishing school was on my mind, I wanted to make it to the NBA. But life had other plans in store for me: I didn't make it to the NBA. I had to learn to live and so I went back to school to finish my class work, eventually earning my B.A.I.S. at Fairleigh Dickinson University. My next dream that inspired this finish was my family.

I was married and I envisioned a good life for my family, so I needed to be in a position to achieve this. When I went to college, I made a promise to myself that I would not raise my kids in the hood because it's too hard to make it out. These visions started out small, but as my belief in myself and my faith grew, I continued to hit my goals. I had a consistent dream – and I won.

I learned that if I didn't try, I would always fail; but if I tried and I never gave up, I would eventually fail my way to the top. It's funny how no one wants to make mistakes. They want to have a smooth run right to the top, but if you don't have experience in solving problems, when you get to the top, you will not be qualified to win.

Being a dreamer in a dreamless society will be a definite challenge for you. If you look and listen closely, stories and remnants of broken dreams are all around you. People will say things like *"why do you want to do that? Is that realistic? No one like us does that."* These comments are designed to plant seeds of doubt in your mind. They give you a quick reason to stop trying and to conform. But do you really want to be like the majority of people who live "normal" lives? The world is looking for some abnormal people, but in a good way. The problems of today are too complex and we need the brightest thinkers and sharpest strategists to move the mountains that hold us back as a society. As the Uncle Sam Poster reads: WE NEED YOU!!!

So get over it. You can't settle in and just be normal, we have enough people like that right now and there's plenty of room at the top, but you have to see it, believe it and pursue it like your mother's life depends on it. Your vision must be treasured. When you treasure something, you will fight for it. Be willing to fight for your dreams, but know that the biggest fight for your dreams will be against yourself. Soon you will find out that you are a creature of habit and you probably have some habits you wish you didn't have. So you have to be committed to waking up every day, looking at yourself in the mirror and facing those challenges that you present to yourself. Know that this is a lifelong process and it will never end, but it will greatly benefit you to pick this fight now.

If you are in an uncomfortable spot right now and things don't look so good in your eyes because of your street address, school, living situation, family background etc., I dare you to cast your vision anyway and believe in it. Someone told me a while ago that all positions in life are temporary. This could be bad or good. If you cast your vision and work for it, you will go on the upward spiral to greatness; but if you do the opposite then you will take the downward spiral to a very predictable life.

"Sight is the enemy of Vision." -Dr. Myles Munroe

You can't trust what you see. This is very practical and requires no faith to attain. Chase what sets your heart on fire. You could finish school, get a job and sacrifice your entire life at a job that isn't part of your purpose. People who live like this are over- worked and underpaid. They are always complaining and probably suffering from depression or anxiety.

When you put a fish in dirt, it'll freak out. Humans are the same way. There is an intended purpose for our lives. If we don't make it to our intended environment, we will struggle in life.

In Alaska, salmon swim upstream to get to the right place to have their babies. To complete this task they must swim upstream against rocks and their bodies are beaten bloody while they swim, jump and dodge hungry bears to get to their destination. I am asking you to take the risk – just as salmon do. Be fearless and take the leap to *your* greatness.

Martin Luther King Jr. envisioned a desegregated country long before it happened. He believed in his dream even though he didn't think he would live to see the fruits of his labor. Look at the results of one man having one vision and acting on it. His DREAM was so powerful that even after he was murdered, his vision lived on. You also have the power inside of you to be a positive influence in the lives of others. When you cast your vision into their hearts, they can live in your dream. Often times, your vision is needed so people can build *their* dreams. By spreading your vision, you can give others the courage and hope to chase their dreams.

Imagine a young black man who is dreaming of going to college, but who is discouraged because blacks aren't allowed to attend colleges in the south. He is on the verge of giving up on his dream when Martin Luther King Jr. marches past him with his vision of hope for a unified future. Now this young man has enough fuel to press through the rhetoric of his present to get to his future. Just as this young man needed King's vision, we need each others' dreams and hopes: we need you to cast yours.

As you cast these dreams, be aware that there will be times in your life when some of the people around you may not have your best interest in mind. For years I lived someone else's dreams. They used my strength, my brain and my athletic ability to live their life. The people who used me in this way were fueled by watching me pursue their dreams for them. During this time in my life, I was suicidal. I thought about killing myself several times and I even attempted a couple of times. I was miserable and I didn't know what to do. This is why I know that when someone is not fulfilling their God-given purpose, it's impossible to be a happy person. People would say to me, *"LaMarqué, you're traveling around the globe and having fun."* My response to that is that I was not living in the vision I had seen since I was a kid. I'd always wanted to preach the gospel, be an entrepreneur, help others and be a community leader. Now that I am walking in this purpose, I am as happy as I have ever been. I feel like I finally have permission to live. But I had to compete against myself.

Due to all the years of living in others dreams, I had to learn how to actually live for me. I learned how to consistently build belief in my dreams and in myself. It was tough at first. I didn't trust myself because all I had ever done was play basketball. I wish I had pursued my vision from the beginning. Although I loved playing basketball and I *did* want to make it to the NBA, I knew it wasn't a part of my purpose. But I pursued it anyway to please others and I suffered because of it.

I can remember how many times I wanted to give up in high school and in college. Although I had a scholarship to play basketball, there were times during that part of my journey when I lost focus on my dream. I was able to press through these issues by continuing to shoot for my dreams.

Yes, I had plenty of issues. I was a teen dad, I hated school and I was struggling to balance my faith with my lifestyle. And I can remember most of the time feeling like a loser, but I never gave up. Instead I would just talk about my dreams all of the time. I never dealt with my reality because I knew I was just passing by. I felt like I was on my way to a better place.

This may seem contradictory, but I had so many issues that I couldn't tackle them all at once. So I dealt with the ones that could hinder me from finishing at that moment. I figured that I would have to eventually face them all as I moved on to the next year or the next level of my life. In doing this, I developed a strategy to deal with my issues. I would speak to my barriers with words like *you will get tired before I will*. To this day, I have never given up on anything because I learned how to overcome and achieve my goals no matter what issue I'm facing. I believe if you just keep working, things go in your favor. But you have to know that you don't win everything right away. Some small losses now may be big victories later. But don't dwell on it. Look at it as a teachable moment and move on.

"Man is anxious to improve their circumstances, but unwilling to improve themselves; they therefore remain bound." - James Allen

I have played basketball my whole life, but during high school I was very nervous and lacked confidence. I even struggled with these issues through my first three years of college. I didn't know how to overcome this mental roadblock until someone spoke to me and said *"the only person who can stop you is you."* This single statement set me free to compete only against myself. If I could outwork myself everyday, who could outwork me?

If I hadn't tackled my low confidence and self-esteem issues, then I wouldn't have been able to accomplish my goals. I had to have my dream in front of me all day and night so that I would have the courage to face my fears. It was a very uncomfortable process for a while, but I got used to the change. To this day, it has been a key principle in my life.

Vision is the picture before the picture. This attribute will most likely be the one thing that gets you through the rough spots that will appear in your life. If you say you have a vision, but you don't believe in it, you will not be able to justify the pain and disappointment of the journey when the test comes; but if you believe in your vision, there will be nothing that can make you give up.

The Farmers Principle

1. Plow the ground
2. Plant good seed
3. Water and feed the seed
4. Pray for the seed
5. Reap the harvest
6. Start all over

In every area of my life, I have followed this process over and over. This is because I believe that everything stems from The Farmer's Principle. If you don't start with preparation, you are prepared to fail. If you follow this process, you will learn that results don't come first. Just like a farmer, you have to believe in what you see: even when you look out and only see five acres of dirt in front of you. Then you start to plow.

Going to school and being a disciplined person is like plowing in the field. No one likes to do it. But if you don't do it, you won't have good ground to put your seed in. The plowing is the most important portion of the process because it is the preparation stage.

As you proceed to chase your dreams, understand there is a process to win at life and you just can't stumble into it. You have to follow the proper steps. It is very sad to really want something so badly that you can see it in your head, but you can't have it in reality because you didn't follow the process.

How big is your vision?

I have a unique vision for my family. When I was growing up in the projects, I told myself that I would not raise my children in that type of environment: I expect them to reach their full potential. I never envisioned myself raising children who had to go through the types of struggles I went through growing up. My idea was to put them in the best environment to help them to win in life. No exceptions!

I teach people that if your dream isn't linked to at least three generations then it isn't big enough. Why would I make such a bold statement? Because life for the average person presents a lot of problems that could easily cause them to give up. If I have larger problems and things become more difficult, it will be easier for me to give up if I only have myself to worry about. But if I am dreaming with my family name on my back and I believe they can't make it without me, this will give me the fuel I need to push through to achieve my greatness. This is a common ancient practice and the principles are still alive today. You may not think you can look three generations deep, but you can. But the first steps are to start thinking about what you want your life to look like, to believe in it and then to chase it down.

Chapter Two Question:

1. What lesson have you learned about VISION from chapter two?

_____
_____
_____
_____

2. Do your actions and your VISION for your life point in the same direction?

_____
_____
_____
_____

3. Do you have a VISION on paper? If not, whose map are you following and to what destination?

_____
_____
_____
_____

Chapter Three: Passion

"Passion is the invisible energy that attracts the supporting cast, which helps pull you to your destiny."- LaMarqué Ward, Sr.

When you hear about passion, you light up. When you see passion, you stand up. To have passion is to have desire—to have a fire that burns within. So why isn't passion embraced anymore? Is it because people are scared of it?

Imagine a young boy who is a little rambunctious in school. His teachers recommend that he be put on medication because he's too active—and that's a problem. His mom is fine with the label because it will calm her son down, but is this always the best solution?

I know all about this scenario: I was that little boy. Thankfully, my mother fought for my right to be great—my right to have passion— and now I am a passionate father, minister, entrepreneur and community leader.

We can't continue to snuff out this fire that burns within. The world needs you to dare to be great and to push the limits. We need you to embrace your passion because the problems of today need a new solution—and the youth of today have to produce it, but you must own your hopes and dreams and really believe in yourself in order to do this.

Know that there will be people who will want to rob you of your passion because they don't have the fortitude to pursue their dreams. Because they haven't embraced their passion, every time you show up, they are smacked in the face with their own lack of resolve. You may notice that all of the criticism you accrue is from people who want you to stay in-line with them. Every time you show a little passion, you move a few steps ahead. What they are really saying is *"please don't leave me behind."* But instead of saying this in a nice way, they attempt to make you feel sad or mad about pursuing your passion. Don't let this discourage you because not everyone feels this way. I believe that my whole existence is based upon your success. If you don't make it, I don't make it. So you must believe in your future– because if you don't believe, no one else can wish you there.

"Chase your passions and life will reward you." – Author unknown

When you chase your passion, your heart is set on fire. When we all chase our passion, the world will have the proper light. You were created to do something great and that thing you were created to do can't be done by anyone else but you.

There are nearly seven billion people in the world and no one has your fingerprint or DNA. Imagine the world without Martin Luther King, Malcolm X, Gandhi, Abraham Lincoln, William Wilberforce or Rosa Parks. They pursued their passion with conviction and honor–and life did reward them. I dare you to be great too.

"You don't have to be the best; you just have to outlast the rest." - LaMarqué Ward, Sr.

Know that you have a lot to believe in: yourself. If there is anyone in the world who deserves to be great, it is you. But with this comes great responsibility. You have to be willing to manipulate your fate with passion and intelligence every single day. This may be much harder than it sounds. When you believe in your dreams and your passion kicks in, inevitably there will be things that will stand in your way. This will probably happen more often than you like, but you have to refuse to give up. When the going gets tough, most people will quit. Don't be most people. Even though everyone has an IQ (I Quit) level, let yours be much higher.

"The leading rule is diligence; leave nothing for tomorrow which can be done today." - Abraham Lincoln

Playing sports is a tough way to make a living. I was told that there would be a one in a million chance that I would make it playing professional basketball. I didn't take heed; instead, I set out on my journey to see what it had to offer me. I worked hard and gave it my all, but I learned very quickly that everyone didn't take it as seriously as I did. Some of the other guys would say that the only thing they wanted out of life was to play basketball. But since these same guys wouldn't work hard in the gym, their actions spoke much louder than their words ever could. The funny thing is that they couldn't understand why they weren't seeing positive results. And inevitably society was blamed for their shortcomings. Don't fall into this trap—at the end of the day YOU are responsible for your own life and the decisions you make. The choices you make today will either set you up or knock you out of position to reach your full potential.

To reach your full potential, you must have passion. Here's the good news: if you live out of your sweet spot, that place inside of you that brings you joy, you'll naturally be passionate. You won't have to make it up because once you believe in yourself; your dreams, disciplines and purpose will begin to align. If you can live from that sweet spot in life, you can do anything. And who can be as passionate as you are about what you desire? What if you are the only person who can deliver in that specific area of gifting? Imagine what life would be like if Thomas Edison hadn't chased his passion— instead of a 60 watt bulb, you might be reading this book by candlelight.

Pioneering: a person or group that originates or helps open up a new line of thought or activity or a new method or technical development.

Our youth today is the first generation to go to college and perform at higher levels. Although it's scary to set out to attain a college degree when you haven't seen many people do it, you need to have the pioneer's mindset.

I love listening to stories about the Gold Rush of the late 1800s when people packed up everything they had and headed west to pursue a better life. Their mere hope and the idea of *"I can make it"* was all they needed to get them going. It fascinates me to listen to stories of how one idea can give people so much energy and hope. When you add desire and the right idea, it is like starting a fire – even when it seems like you are the only one doing so.

Young people today have to understand that it's OK to feel like you are alone sometimes. It's OK if you don't always have someone to follow in the right direction. You have to know that it is your destiny to rewrite the handbook of your journey. You are the author of your manual. Your destiny is so great, no one else can lead you to the level in which you are going. This is not an insult to our elders—it's just that in these times, we need ideas, people and concepts that have never been brought forth. We need more trailblazers.

I was the first person to do a lot of things in my family and I am grateful to God for my success. As I continue to leap onto new levels, I don't feel so alone because I am running into more pioneers who are headed in the same direction. Stay on the road until you get to your destination and remember that a pioneer takes risks, believes and never gives up.

"I would rather die chasing the impossible than to live in the predictable."--Author unknown

Find out what you will need to do in order to reach your goal and then make those habits your everyday habits. Start your personal trip today and don't worry about what everyone else thinks, but follow your heart and will it to come true.

Brainstorm: Take two minutes to write down everything that comes to mind when you hear the word SUCCESS:

_____
_____
_____
_____
_____
_____
_____
_____
_____

1. When you think about these words, do you smile and is your heart on fire? Yes /No

2. Would you do this for free if you could? Yes/No

3. What great person in history mastered your dream? Have you studied their process? Yes/No

Chapter Four: Character

"Integrity is the silent ego that will speak for you when you're long gone." -LaMarqué Ward, Sr.

Character is the foundation on which you build your house. Would you build your house on a cracked foundation? Then why would you take the chance of building your future on a cracked foundation? Character is who you are when no one is looking. Are you challenging yourself in the areas of character at home, school or through your work ethic?

A young lady once shared something with me that her teacher told her: *"How you do anything is how you do everything."* This reminded me of the time I went to a teacher's conference in Myrtle Beach. Although only three people showed up, I was still committed to teach my workshop as if there were 5,000 people in the room. I started on time, ended on time and I still took questions from those few people. And as a result, they shared their gratitude for my passion. You have to remember that you never know who you are in front of – and if you change depending on the size of the crowd, you are not being authentic.

You want to always be the same person, filled with character, no matter the situation.

Having character is the act of remaining consistent in certain behaviors or beliefs. This is also the root to trust. People trust you when they see you are consistent in the proper behaviors. When you are growing up and your parents put certain restrictions on you like curfew or driving limitations, these are tests to see if you can handle more responsibility. If you pass these tests, then you will, naturally, inherit more trust and grow in responsibility. And having the proper character, even at a young age, will protect you and position you on the road to success in ways you may have never thought about.

I have a friend who is 10 years younger than me who is a manager at a major phone company in Cincinnati. At the age of 21, he ran for a position on the school board for Cincinnati Public Schools, while managing a million dollar budget at work. Just one year later, he received a promotion with more pay and responsibility. Did he ask for more money or did he earn more trust? He did it the right way. When you do it with character, you'll do it the right way too.

Good Character is like putting an umbrella up in the rain. It protects you from the elements. If you want to challenge yourself in any area of your life, allow character and integrity to guide your decisions. When you begin to be lead only by what's ethically right, then you allow yourself to be put in position to win long- term in life. And the younger you are when you apply these principles, the sooner the results will come. But remember: this principle alone will not take you to the top, but if you combine character with passion and vision, you can use this as the key to unlock the door of your destiny.

During my life, I have witnessed various examples of good character. My high-school coach was a very passionate man who was driven to motivate and help young men reach their goals. He was consistent in so many areas. Not only would he encourage us not to give up, but he made us dig deep into our personal lives to become self-sufficient. He taught us to be a doer and not just a talker. He would hold us accountable on every hand. He would not allow us to hide behind our poor habits. We even began to apply these principles when we were at home. Coach T's motto was *"Never let anyone out-work you."* On our basketball team, it was our staple. We played defense like no one else and we finished the season on a 19-1 run and almost won a state title.

Coach T's work ethic had spilled over into our personal lives and it became one of our character traits. He made us believe that the only way we could achieve greatness was by out-working and out- witting our opponents. We couldn't see it at the time, but our manhood was being molded – and it was awesome. Back then we didn't realize the value of Coach T's efforts: he was building the blocks to our future, one block at a time. Some of us became good excuse makers in the process, but others rose to the challenge and delivered. As I look back, I can now see the ones who did what was required of them to ensure they would meet their goals and I realize the important role that character played in our lives.

To this day, I love this coach so much for teaching me to never let anyone bring me down. This same principle can apply in your life as well. If you just keep moving forward, the rest will take care of itself. And know that what you want out of life is not as far away from you as you may think it is, but you will need to work on YOU first. If you do this, you will somehow find yourself closer to your dreams.

"Leadership is the capacity and will to rally men and women to a common purpose and the character which inspires confidence." - Barnard Montgomery, British Field Marshall

People are already in position to help you, but you have to help them believe in you. Character aides you in this process. Once you have earned credibility because of your consistent good nature, you have won them over. Now you can capitalize on those relationships. Only then will they vouch for you, write that reference letter or make that introduction to the friend. I can remember reading a passage in my favorite book that says *"I want you to prosper as your soul prospers."* I could not understand this wisdom until I was older: you have to improve yourself internally before you can prosper externally. This doesn't mean you won't see people, who have weak character, gain wealth and notoriety. They may seem like they are living a prosperous life, but chances are it will be temporary if it's not built on character.

Tiger Woods followed this process to the letter. He had a vision for his life and had the desire to accomplish it, but because of a character flaw, his life was flipped upside down. He lost his wife and was probably hurting beyond measure. In times like this, you find out what men are really made of. Woods went away, worked on himself and came to grips with his issues and is now competing in life as well as on the golf course. I love the fact that he didn't give up and that he is working his life out as if it were an open book, but I believe he is a good example of what not to do in life.

"I watch what people say and I listen to what they do." - LaMarqué Ward, Sr.

Having good character is the difference between just having the potential to achieve your goals and actually accomplishing your goals. It is also the difference between choosing a good behavior over a less favorable one, as listed here:

Promiscuity	Self-control
Discipline over eating	Healthy living
Poor language	Good communication skills
Poor attendance	Desire
Disruptive	Strong vision

The choices listed on the right may seem a little tougher at first, but these are the choices that will set you up to win in life. And the good thing about character is that it's never too late to build on it. You just have to make the decision to accept the challenge of building yourself from within.

Chapter Four Questions:

1. What does character mean to you?

_____
_____
_____
_____

2. How will living a life with character position you for a bright future?

_____
_____
_____
_____

3. Is character popular in today's culture? Yes/No - Why or why not?

_____
_____
_____
_____

Chapter Five: You vs You

"Whoever has your ear has your destiny." - Chuck Futel

In the game of life we surrender so much of our power to others, but we don't realize it until we attempt to gain independence. If you choose to follow the crowd, it will come at a cost. It took me years to regain the power I gave up to others. I chose to be a follower when I started engaging in risky behaviors like sex, drugs and alcohol. But because my friends were doing it, I thought it was cool. The results, however, were very uncool: court dates, hurt and pain. The price I paid was huge, but you have an opportunity to avoid the mistakes that I made by refusing to surrender your mental strength to others. Your battle in life is already challenging enough —and that's when it's just you! You have to learn to create your own identity, with your discipline, vision, passion and character, from within. This will cause you to begin to live life out of *your* purpose and not out of the thoughts and ideas of others.

When you are tested by peer pressure, there are two things you should do. First, imagine the consequences of your actions. Do you think the results will be something you will be proud of? Second, don't be afraid to say no. You don't always have to do what everyone else is doing. If you can grasp these concepts early on, you will be in position to lead yourself to a fruitful destiny.

This won't be easy. It will take courage to stand your ground, but you will begin to see results. In this life it's so easy to do the wrong thing, but you have to learn how to get in your own way so you can stay on track. You will need to learn your own habits. By learning your habits, you can make the proper adjustments in your daily disciplines. This will position you to resist temptation and to win consistently.

For example, if you have tried alcohol, but you don't want to drink it anymore then you might not want to go to that party where you know there will be drinks and you will be tempted. Or if you are dating and you don't want to be intimate before it's your time, make it a group date. If you can't make the group date happen, then don't allow yourself to be in a secluded place in a one-on- one situation. This will give you a good chance to keep your dignity.

These are just two examples of the many situations you may face. But if you think about these situations ahead of time, you won't be caught off guard when you are faced with them. You have the courage to say no in any of these situations. Just remember that every choice you make is a seed sown for either a hopeless existence or a bright future – and you have the right to choose which one.

Your habits and your habits alone will demote or promote you – so why would you consistently make decisions based on what others want you to do? As you move through the stages of life, you want to be free to move around with *your* plans, goals and ideas and not someone else's. Don't get me wrong – I'm not saying don't listen to anyone; they just need to be the right people. It took me some time to break free from the influence of other's thoughts and ideas for my life, but now I am living *my* dream of helping others build their dreams.

When you are attempting to move forward with your life and chase your dreams and goals, you have to believe you can achieve them. Don't allow fear, doubt and unbelief to dominate your thoughts. Try this instead: think about going for you goal with everything you've got. Then imagine yourself not making it. Now imagine yourself getting up, dusting yourself off and starting over with a new plan to reach your goal. Did you notice that when you thought about not making your goal, you were still breathing and your heart was still beating? Life will go on when you make mistakes or fall short of some of your goals, but you have to train your mind to get back up, start planning and move forward again.

"Life is a series of daily practices for a few big events." LaMarqué Ward, Sr.

The world needs you. Do you believe that? If you say you believe it, what do your actions say? I know the world needs you and I dare you to go for it. Be the only one to leave the group and reach for the stars. You just might be the first star of many to follow. The world needs you to believe in yourself. Start by chasing *your* passion and being a leader – not a follower. And never forget: if you don't make it, we can't make it. So start now and let greatness be your inspiration. Never stop running until you have reached your destiny – and then start over with a new goal. Remember, although life is a competition, you CAN make it. But first you must start to compete with you against YOURSELF. Make this your lifestyle.

Chapter Five Questions:

1. What areas of strength have you surrendered by not having the courage to be different?

_____
_____
_____
_____

2. When you think about confronting your poor habits, how do you feel?

_____
_____
_____
_____

3. What barriers can stop you from reaching your goals?

_____
_____
_____
_____

4. How will you overcome those barriers?

_____
_____
_____
_____

For more information:

www.dreambuildersuniversity.com

www.competingasalifestyle.com

On Twitter: @DreamBuilderCEO

On Facebook: Competing As A Lifestyle You vs You

Competing as a Lifestyle
You vs. You
Edited by:
Desiré Bennett

35418642R00024

Made in the USA
Middletown, DE
10 February 2019